Chimes

Whisper

Silence

**Poems by
Robert C. Covel**

Vabella Publishing
P.O. Box 1052
Carrollton, Georgia 30112

©Copyright 2020 by Robert C. Covel

All rights reserved. No part of the book may be reproduced or utilized in any form or by any means without permission in writing from the author. All requests should be addressed to the publisher.

Cover design by Alistair Riddoch

The poems "Singularity" and "Intimations of Mortality" appeared in Exit 271, Summer 2016.

The poems "Rose of Sharon," "Twilight of the Gods," and "Krishna and the Milkmaids" appeared in the novel "Twilight of the Gods, Vabella Publishing, 2018.

Manufactured in the United States of America

13-digit ISBN 978-1-942766-71-1

Library of Congress Control Number 2020940905

10 9 8 7 6 5 4 3 2 1

Dedication

To my wife Deloris.

For her price is far above rubies.

Table of Contents

Epigraph	1
1969	2
Temporality	4
Ars Mathematica	5
Babel On	7
Bibliophiliac	8
Diminuendo	9
Epiphany	10
Fall Planting	11
Fanfare for Graduation	12
Festival of Lights	13
Haiku	
gold	14
breeze	15
pine tree	16
breath	17
butterfly	18
hesitant	19
dust	20
here	21
café mocha	22
violin	23
rain	24
outbuilding	25
waves	26
zen paradox	27
leaf	28
wabi sabi	29
loss	30
crimson	31
web	32

Hollywood: the Stars	33
Iconoclasts	34
Intimations of Mortality	36
Leaf	38
What Dreams May Come	39
Listening to Chocolate	40
Dry Heat	41
The Truth of Suffering	42
Love Is the Heart of Home	43
Flicker	45
Mind Meld	46
Nihil Obstat	47
Numbers	48
Obit	50
Outside Inside	52
Pas de Deux Engagement	53
Photo Stream/Funeral	54
The Point	56
Problems of Translation	58
Relative Birthday	59
Rome, the Eternal	60
Seasonal	63
Seismic	64
Silver	65
Singularity	66
Stage Four	67
Winter: Two Poems	69
The Burden of Beauty	71
Mediterranean by Moonlight	72
Gold	73
Danse	74
Getting Back to Normal	75
Rose of Sharon	77

Twilight of the Gods	79
Krishna and the Milkmaids	81
Still	82
Fourth Dementia	83
Design	84
Arachne	86
ἔκστασις	87
Sign of Loss	89
Electric Blue	91
Loss and Memory	93
Knapping Stones	94
Now and Zen	96
Food for Thought	97
Drift	98
On the Inevitability of Entropy	99
Spring Morning after Rain: Impressions	100
Solstice	101
I Am Bic	102
Maternity	103
Abject	105
Guernica	106
Tunnel Visions	107
Three Score and Ten	109

Epigraph

Face the wall and breathe

Thoughts drift up like incense smoke

Chimes whisper silence

1969

Nostalgia for a Flower Child from a different century,
now resident of the suburbs of the memories
of the Woodstock Generation,
I sit, eyes closed, strains of music
echo in my head from ear to ear.
Reminiscences shimmer, softened edges
smoothed by the passing of the years,
selective amnesiac images filter out
harsher dissonances of reality.

Before freak flag was dropped to half mast,
surrendering to age, and peace
 and love were bartered
to greed of capitalism
for middle class security;
before needle tracks and tears
inducted Jim, Jimi, and Janis
charter members of the Twenty-Seven Club;
before dreams of peace and love dissipated
like a drifting cloud of Ganja smoke,
as the battles in the rice paddies,
the streets of Watts and Chicago
gave way to détente and compromise;
before drum beats gave way to tick of time
and Baby Boomers settled in
to Medicare and mediocrity,
before it all--
the child danced, a swirl of flowing hair,
of beads and bell bottoms,
a dervish before the altar of rock and roll.

Behind lines and wrinkles in the mirror,
behind dimming eyes and failing ears,
limbs slowed by touch of time,
the child still pirouettes and leaps,
behind the Piper's notes,
 the sound track of his youth still plays,
and calls the tune,
notes and swirls of sound
still charm his feet
to prance down the golden path,
back to the Garden again.

Temporality

Christmas Eve, against a sepia thatch,
ragged leaves sprawl to solstice sun.
A slender stem, delicate coiffure tousled,
dances winsome before the wanton wind,
trembles: seeds release, drift to rest and wait.

New Year's Eve, the turn of time
ticks; another bloom bursts a blaze
uplifted, petals flaunt a petulant gold.
Beside, a withered stem sprawls,
 spent, its seeds, glory gone.

The little death, release and ecstasy.
Moments, lives float, fragile blooms
Pass, pass on, the past
Exhales, expires, a puff of wind
that bears a whispered note to time.

Ars Mathematica

Cerebral art of integers combines,
equations dance in balanced elegance
of sides and angles, ratios that plot the stars.
The order of inductive patterning,
the scores, the notes that scale the universe.

Pythagoras, Euclid, Fibonacci:
artists of the mind,
reveal order, patterns:
ratios, internal harmonies,
Golden Mean,
the secret chord of the universe attuned.

Theme and variations, fractals,
Fibonacci sequences,
from elegant precisions
to subtle mysteries of Pi
repeating beyond counting
irrational but rational,
numbers improper, imaginary
though real, stretching limits,
measuring unmeasured.

Beyond the sweep of clouds,
murmuring of ocean's whispering waves;
beyond the continental drift,
dance of life, the flow of impermanence
from quantum mysteries
to swirling waltz of galaxies
of space-time choreographies.

Beneath rhythms,
of music, poetry, and art,
the mathematics resonate--serene, composed
equations, beyond emotion's dissonance.
Inscribing ratios on irrationality,
solving for the variables, the limits of infinity.

Babel On

Like the mythic builders, confounded
by the chaos of un-comprehended noise:
vocabulary, enunciation, syntax
a jumble, jarring sounds.
We translate verses, stories,
shout across the chasm,
meanings lost in translations,
sounds dispersed, wafted, distorted.
No equivalencies, A cannot equal B;
Alpha is not Omega.
Hieroglyphics to demotic Greek,
Rosetta maps uncertain patterns.

Linguistics, semiotics flicker like candles
in Lascaux caverns, Paleolithic mindset
in images, enigmatic shapes without grammar,
lexicon lost across eons.
Vowels and consonants,
sibilants, clicks, and grunts,
cuneiform and alphabets--
we babble on our meanings, found and lost.

Bibliophiliac

Marshaled on shelves in rows,
titles facing out, spines straight,
rows of books await inspection.
But from within neat printed pages, the voices,
a mute cacophony—
ideas and emotions,
calmly structured arguments or wild irrational rants
seduce the mind, the eye, the touch.

From innocence of childhood
the whispering rhymes
of fairy tales, Mother Goose,
enchant, entrance with once-upons and ever-afters.
The cubby hole, the book nook
where treasured friends awaited,
pages caressed, fondled, sharing lives:
growing ideas and worlds,
the dreams and memories of youth.

Book stores and dim-lit libraries,
among the stacks with ancient tomes,
intoxicating fragrances of leather and old paper,
the polyglot of tongues, word hoard, whisper
their wisdom, poetry of cultures' myths and legends.
Voices of sages, shamans, and bards,
enigmatic as the Sybil,
sing their enticing siren song.

Diminuendo

Struggle, quiet tension wrestling with the unseen,
grappling as muscles tense, release,
cling, to fight inevitability.
Release, relief-- muscles relax.

Hands that held and soothed,
now palms up, resigned.
Lips that smiled, kissed, and spoke
surrender in mute silence.

The Potter's shaped vessel now empty,
contents gone, dispersed
as Form reverts to Formlessness
in shards of shattered clay.

We who remain as witnesses hover
useless before the great Mystery,
before the great unanswered question,
caught between loss and hope.

The final breath, Spiros now released, the whisper
like final notes, final strains
of life diminishing, pass through the room,
drift up and out to fade unheard, to silence.

Epiphany

Season's end, a January night,
last decorations glow
beneath bleak-black winter sky.
Death rattle of oak leaves rustle,
polar wind-sweep touches skeletal branches.
Above, the opalescent moon rides
drifting clouds.
Beyond, awesome awe-ful distances
where stars burn cold,
apparent patterns on the vault of sky.

No guiding light to lead Magi--
perceived order, structure
of intelligent design—
or randomness, blankness, chaos, and entropy?
Stars blink back askance.

Fall Planting
(For Shelly Murphy and James Hopkins)

Beneath the honey glaze of late September sun
chrysanthemums give back gleaming gold
of drifting swallowtails
as aster petals twinkle pastel hues.
Hummingbirds and fumbling bees search out
the final fleeting sips
before dregs of winter's bitter brew.

Terra cotta pots swath tender roots
in rich dark soil, cradle autumn's temporary blooms,
reminders of our frail impermanence,
as pansies' upturned faces seek the distant sun.
Beneath raised beds the dormant bulbs
of tulips, hyacinths, and daffodils
drowse beneath the mulch,
deep dreams of spring and life revived.

Daylilies, diurnal, flame and die,
their fleeting beauty flashes and departs.
More durable perennials, dependable as seasons' shift,
cycle and recycle with the sun,
turning and returning,
enduring strength
from raised beds to wakening renewed.

Fanfare for Graduation
(For Morgan Hebert)

The culminating moments of our lives
dawn bright as sunlight touching polished brass,
awakening the birds to morning song.
Divergent notes entwine in harmonies
that drift like clouds and float across the breeze.

As notes flow into melodies, combine,
the point and counterpoint of days' events
blend and coalesce to symphonies.
As movement follows movement, tempos change,
adagio, allegro, shifting moods
with swirl of strings, crescendo-ing of brass
with flitting songs of woodwinds woven through.
The trumpet notes rise clear, a clarion call
above the vital pulse of tympani.

The order of our lives, composed, connects
with unheard harmonies: the Absolute
is shadowed forth in unity of sound.
With pomp and circumstance we celebrate
the grand procession toward the Greater Mind.

Festival of Lights

Twinkling Christmas lights and gleam of ornaments,
Menorah's flickering flame, the candles' glow,
the soothing warmth of Yuletide fire--
destroyed by muzzle flash and pipe bomb burst.

Still searching, trinity of faiths from Father Abraham--
culture becomes occult, then cult.
The lamp unto our feet, that guides
our human-ness, is dimmed, replaced
by threat of darkness visible.

And those who kneel, or bow, or sit, prostrate themselves
before the One, the Way, the Tao,
are trampled into mortal dust
of those who will not see.

Haiku

Gold ray gilds cloud-drift,
calls forth one shimmering note.
Trees stand forth: sun rise.

Breeze stills, ripples clear.
Leaf floats on clouds, swallows soar
on deep clarity.

Pine tree: spent cones hang,
one green cone, new seeds concealed.
Needles glisten, morning sun.

Quiet breath exhaled,
heart beats, quiet, steady flow.
Incense smoke ascends.

Orange butterfly
fumbles over fading blooms.
Yellow leaf drifts down.

Uncertain eyes gaze.
Hesitant footsteps stumble.
Infant once again.

Feather duster, broom—
reminded that thou art dust—
fighting entropy.

No one is from here.
No one can ever stay here.
There is no "here" here.

Café mocha steam
rises toward October clouds:
morning mists disperse.

Gleaming violin,
strings vibrate in honeyed tones:
mind in harmony.

Sunday morning rain
Patters golden leaves, its text
Like a whispered prayer.

Outbuilding leans, drunk
with time, adoring vines tug
walls to leaf-mould bed.

Diamond-shimmer waves,
swirling breeze wafts drifting leaves
warmed by waning sun.

Zen Quote, wash your bowl,
Young boy says there is no spoon:
Truth in paradox.

Fan-shaped yellow leaf
flutters, hesitant to fall:
to end or begin.

Leaf on fresh cement
proves, disproves impermanence:
abstract in concrete.

Half-eaten treat left,
chew toy awaits, un-retrieved:
images of loss.

Crimson leaves, like flames,
flicker, drift with clouds, reflect
three worlds, shifting forms.

Long legs still, suspend,
the moment is, caught, uncaught:
web of space and time.

Hollywood: the Stars

Flash of cameras, evanescent burst
of lights illuminates the night.
Cinematic world in abeyance,
a freeze-frame moment celebrates
artifice captured on strips of film.
Stepping forth from limousines,
Olympian in demeanor, stars
tread the crimson path,
diamond-glitter constellations
adorning wrists and milky throats.
Dramatic pause and pose,
flashing smiles for fans,
their adoration offered up
as tribute to iconic shadows of the Real.

Glitterati disappear
within the sanctum, to celebrate
the moment of adulation
of golden figures posed.
Crowds disperse to darkness
of ordinary lives.

Above hills and street lights,
above the vaunted sign
ensconced, beyond the scene,
quiet velvet night, though blotted out
by incandescent glow, descends.
The cosmic swirl, the Milky Way
drifts through space and time.
Indifferent to honors or adoration,
untold trillions, points of light
of stars and galaxies
flicker, constellations pirouette
silent majesty.

Iconoclasts

"The best lack all conviction, while the worst
Are full of passionate intensity." –William Butler Yeats

Rabid hordes bent on destruction,
driven by passion and ideology,
they wield the torch, the ax, the sledge
against art and artifacts.
Armies sweep like locusts, devouring,
leaving parched earth, red rock,
desolation of cultural genocide.

Bonfires blaze as sparks like tongues of flame
swirl upward; leather, vellum, and paper burn.
Calligraphy, the scrawl of ink, whispers across the page,
as thought, belief, and feeling are silenced by the torch,
the words made ash, burnt offering
of impassioned brute believers.

The images of Gautama,
Bemiyan Buddhas step forth
freed, delivered from clefts of desert stone.
Carved by hands now dust,
shattered, crushed by hurtful hands,
thus dust cast down to dust,
proving impermanence.

Now victims of iconoclasts
denying culture, history
as they shatter faces of faceless gods
in the name of a faceless god.

Shattered shards of culture now litter
museum floors and desert sands,
cast down by brutish hands.
But beyond their reach in realms of abstract purity,
faceless faces of feelings, thoughts
look down with perfect equanimity.
Iconoclasts cast down, shattered into dust,
swept before the winds of time.

Intimations of Mortality

Spinal procedure,
laminectomy,
fusion--L4 and L5,
one pain replaces another.
The hurt of healing
becomes the new ab/normal.

At night to sleep, perchance disturbed,
by needle-wielding blood seekers.
Stretched, and attached to a rack,
hooked to oxygen and monitors,
the patient poked, prodded, and stuck:
impaled by needles, IV drip,
while a clipboard-bearing pilgrim
attends to the mystery of numbers,
life-supporting functions reduced
to BP, temp and oxygen.
Coiled in the recliner, sleep-deprived,
in tortured fetal pose,
I watch the retinue appear, depart.
Our new confines, Spartan comfort,
one flower print the sole décor,
the furnishings: one bed and one reclining chair.
Our space, our lives upturned,
shrunk to this little measure,
diurnal monotony.

Sound track, voices from on high,
 intercom above the medical routine,
 tinkling lullaby from the maternity,
 pleasant interlude announces birth,
and then "Code Blue, Room 203,"
 darker note in minor key.
Death and entrances,
swirl of mortality
cycled and recycled
through mundane moments.

Nurses, doctors, caretakers—
 helping, healing, but
helpless in the struggle
against the icy touch,
cold visitor not quite
kept at bay

Leaf

Veined web, network of memories,
unsubstantial, fragile at rest.
Cells return to soil,
green to brown.
From spring to fall, the sun's diurnal path
has measured out its days,
giving life and light to chloroplasts.
Now-dead stems drew life
from soil to which they return.

Once-verdant emerald bud turns dark,
fulfilled by time,
plucked as it faced upward
and followed a star that counted its days,
from green to goldengrove to earth tones,
the palette of life's spectrum.
In my hand the remains of the day, a delicate tracery:
I look for life in veins.

What Dreams May Come

Midnight universe,
images flash across clouds of sleep,
jagged bolts among synapses.
Nightmares run down canyons of memory,
galloping down dreamscape.
Dali-esque collages, faces and events,
shadowed realities, surreal
on Plato's cave wall, half-remembered,
full of sound and flurry of images,
dance behind eyelids.

Past and present flicker behind REM sleep.
Random patterns, connected disconnect,
riverrun past Eve and Adam's,
past Freud to images
that are Jung once only.
Time melts and flows,
contracts and ripples on itself,
temporal, temporary
as sleep becomes Wake-fulness.
Midnight universe is skull-shaped.

Listening to Chocolate

Exercise in mindfulness,
single Hershey's chocolate--
like attentive novices, they bow
before the offering:
Lilliputian volcanic silver cone,
labeled plume of smoke
wavers before their breath.

Details noted, regard the morsel,
feeling weightless mass
in Brobdignagian hands
then lift it to attentive ears.

Fingers caress the wrapper,
unveiling luscious form.
Whispered sensuality entices silken sigh
endorphin flow.
Dusky curves and fragrance
raised finally to waiting lips.

On the tongue, a communion of sweetness
melts and yields to gentle bites,
giving itself unwrapped.
Eyes closed, in raptured pleasure--
The mindful moment's afterglow
whispers to the soul.

Dry Heat

No rain, just sun and heat—
hot pump handle,
a trickle from the spout, precious to the touch.
Bucket gapes to sip the drops,
life of water's splash.
Wind vane stands—still—
Blades outstretched in vain.

Heat-shimmer rises from the dirt
that sifts and shifts between our toes.
The hound insensate on the porch,
too hot to pant.

She watches, gasping, hand to parched throat,
pondering the cloudless sky
blue, but not the blue of water
but of drought
for water is the life.

The Truth of Suffering

By the road, a hunched communion,
buzzards settle and flap,
bowing before roadkill offering—
rabbit or possum or coon.
They flutter, uneasy at traffic flow,
then settle to offal repast,
a feast of suffering.

I stop at a red light, news absorbs me
as a cardinal fluffs before the wind,
by a leaf of a sapling branch.
Beneath, a man huddles,
smudged flag and illegible name patch on the dirty jacket
grimy hand outstretched.
He offers an illegible cardboard sign,
its message etched behind his eyes.
A dollar extended from my window,
a moment of contact, touching and touched.
A horn blows behind. The light has changed.

The cardinal flits before me.
In my mirror, a face and raised hand
offer hopeless gratitude.
His suffering recedes in silvered glass
as I make the turn toward home.

Love Is the Heart of Home
(based on a musical composition by Andrew F. Poor)

A house is made of plaster,
of wood and glass and stone,
the haven that we come to
to rest after we roam.

A place with loving family
where we never feel alone,
a house is just a building,
but love is the heart of home.

REFRAIN:
The warm embrace of loving arms
enfolds the memories we've known.
The place may shelter from the storm,
but love is the heart of home.

Our memories of childhood,
of joys we've shared and sorrows known
with family and loved ones
because love is the heart of home.

REFRAIN:
Throughout the years, through sun and storm,
the constant love through clouds has shown.
The gold beyond the rainbow's end:
for love is the heart of home.

REFRAIN
When our lives on earth are ended,
our spirits gone, our lives outgrown:
we are never separated,
for our love is the heart of home.

REFRAIN:
The warm embrace of loving arms
enfolds the memories we've known.
The place may shelter from the storm,
but love is the heart of home.
Love is the heart of home.

Flicker
(For David Rain Beverly)

The candle flame ignites the incense glow,
as fragrant plume drifts upward with my breath.
The whispered waft of bamboo flute enfolds
the silence like a cloud—it flows and shifts.

As glow reduces the incense stick to ash,
I sit—and watch—the wick and wax, the flame
consumes itself; as notes reverberate
to silence--that the darkness comprehends.

Mind Meld

My head on the pillow, clock ticks
synchronized to heart beats.
My mind, out of time
and space flows and melts,
melds in persistent memories.
Connections disconnect and reconnect,
pastiche of past and present:
symbols and images
as matter flows to energy
and dark to light.

On bedside table, silenced
to insentience, smartphone rests
unplugged, turned off,
entangled in a web:
Digital dreams among circuits,
influx of images and emotions,
electrons stream collective consciousness.
Internet REM--
Received Electronic Messages--
from the Gestalt of AI.
Rants, diatribes, manifestos
confessions awaiting absolution
or affirmations stream into the repository
awaiting a response.

Mind returns to time and space
and conscious intellect. Hand reaches
for the phone, streaming messages await.
Fingertips connect and meld
with circuitry, receiving signals
from the web.
Fingers play like harp strings,
in touch with sympathetic vibration
of Universal Mind.

Nihil Obstat
(for Alan Watts)

Zero is not nothing; circumference
circumscribes a concept,
encompasses a reality.
Nihilism, a concept of nothing,
is not nothing.
The concept of nothing permeates.

Before the beginning was the un-comprehended darkness
and from the void, from nothing, everything.
Light burst forth from the Abyss,
unmoved mover.

In dark spaces between our dreams,
nothing haunts our thoughts.
In the void of space between stars,
impermanence flows
upon the face of the deep.
Nothing is perfect.
Nothing lasts forever.
Our nada who art in nada.
Nada es perfecto.
Nothing does not offend.

Numbers

Complex equations of a calculate life,
taxonomies of meaning
and functions:
systole and diastole, iambic beats, metronome:
the pulses of a period
measuring the flux
through moments, days, and years.

Legions quantify phenomena,
sub atomic particles,
quarks charmed and colored,
bosons beyond mass,
beyond the limits of rationality.
Search for unity
of tiny and immense,
theories of everything
within uncertainty.

Cosmos-swirl,
vortex of equations,
parsecs measured in seconds,
tick of relative time.
Calculator buttons that click
like prayer beads tallying mumbled mantras,
whisper of sand grains in a glass,
developing an algorithm
for structure of a cloud.

Irrational and imaginary,
Pi times square root of minus one,
divided by zero, undefined
though not unimagined.
God or gods or scientists
in a cosmic casino,
counting cards or betting on a wheel,
click of dice,
they cast the rattled bones,
betting in a zero-sum game.

Obit

Second-cup Sunday morning ritual,
coffee and croissant
the world's events unfold
in black and white.
Headlines above the fold,
sports scores and game details.
Then cartoons:
frames in primary colors,
two-dimensional humor
in simple golden worlds unchanging.

Thus inoculated, I turn the page.
"Obituary" should be in Gothic script.
Arranged against the chaos of mortality,
the careful pattern of each entry.
I look at pictures--
a dark halo, impermanence unseen.
Old and young, each hopeful face,
some, outdated poofy hair,
chosen by grieving families.
Text: the facts and memories,
birth and expiration dates,
ordered in a pattern,
catalogues of survivors, a summary of life's events,
sometimes cause of death,
and final arrangements like a tolling bell.

Behind careful order, randomness,
lives that spun like a roulette wheel,
flashing red and black,
days on the calendar, events celebrated:
birthdays, anniversaries, holidays.
For each one day that passes by each year,
not marked in black, but waiting.
Wheel spun by Fortune's ghastly hand,
ball bounces, caroming as days and years pass,
all bets are in, until the number's called

and we cash in our chips.

I fold the paper, take a final lukewarm sip,
and turn to crossword puzzle clues.
I fill in letters in a pattern, complete the random task.
I hear a distant echo,
click of a turning wheel.

Outside Inside

Eyes closed, hands settled on the lap,
Quiet breath flows outside and in.
Inner darkness of the settled mind
ripples, connecting silence, all to all.

And after, looking up at points of light
that blaze beyond, immensity of mind
that stretches out from body
 locked in time and space.

Orion rises sideways over trees,
fortuitous arrangement: distant suns,
four dimensions flat, reduced to two,
space-time backlit by dawn-glow, harbinger of fall.

Arbitrary moments, perceived as somehow real,
snapshot held, the flow of temporality,
connections made beyond impressions,
physics and metaphysics unified,
the inner and the outer with the breath.

Pas de Deux Engagement
(for Emi and Alex)

Music rises, gentle harmony
that lifts two hearts, the flow
and pirouette of dancers, limbs intertwined:
the yin and yang
uplifting and uplifted,
a waltz swirl across the floor.
As music pauses, fades,
diminuendo of movement,
quiet intensity of the moment.
The genuflection, proffered gem
on a circle of perfect gold.

Dance becomes an overture,
prelude of a life, love in harmony:
Departures and returns—
Swirl, pause—
Embrace, release.
Spinning revolutions of two lives,
circles within circles.
Blessed, honored by the Muse of Dance,
the choreography of love,
music and dance, the metaphor
of rhythms shared,
aesthetics of the art of love.

Photo Stream/Funeral

Big screen HD, soothing backdrop music,
streams photos, black and white,
pre-Kodachrome.
Images with creased and tattered edges,
 retrieved from coffee-table albums,
cookie tins, shoe boxes, then digitized
and organized to recall a loved one's life.

Images slide into place—
memories of holidays with gifts and food,
the decorated trees and laden tables,
children open gifts, uncertain smiles snapped
in place, frozen on the screen.
Adult faces caught and held,
women clutching purses, pill box hats
perched on pin-curled hair,
Men in tilted fedoras with dangling cigarettes,
staring at camera lens.
Upturned lips, half smiles
belie the desperation in their eyes.

Times and places, captured faces,
some known and some anonymous,
seem somehow known,
archetypal visages,
a photo stream flowing back
to Matthew Brady and daguerreotypes.
Sepia tones, to black and white,
the flow of life and space-time,
frozen, held,
reduced to two dimensions.

Fragmented pictures and memories
stream across the screen,
a life once lived and gone,
but held, digitized into a loop
that turns on itself,
a mobius strip of images,
symbol of something like eternity.

The Point

On Sistine Chapel's ceiling
God's hand extends
a proffered gesture,
the touch of the divine,
charged with giving life.

Index finger pointed,
three others folded back,
thumb upward, cocked,
pudgy hand a weapon
in toddler's un/innocent, imitative play.

Adult hands extend, to indicate,
point out, select:
unmannerly but innocent.
Manual metaphor stabs the air
to make a point
charged with rhetoric
to threaten or accuse,
one finger forward,
three self-condemning fingers back.

The message escalates,
fingers, thumb replaced
with deadly force
of steel and lead,
the pointed metaphor
now mortality.

Human hands extend:
accuse, console,
caress or hit,
to love or loathe,
the hands that give or take.
From innocence of child's games
to angry stabbing point-blank threats,
single digit outthrust to prove
the point of life or death.

Problems of Translation

Lotus blossoms drift on placid ponds,
petals upward, floating clouds,
contemplating, a dream of self
that separates.
A summer breeze lifts pollen,
a code of DNA whispers in the air,
transferred, translated into fertile dreams
of fruit and life.
The message cast like dust before the wind,
chaos-controlled, butterfly wing-wafted,
determines the drift of procreation.
Deep beneath, roots embed in ooze,
preconscious, still un-imaged, unimagined,
dark dreams unified,
float upward to the light,
the Logos undefined.

Relative Birthday

An arbitrary moment passes,
a number of rotations, revolutions,
of a planet around a star,
a period filled with events
for one sentient being,
one among billions across the eons.
The thoughts, the joys and sorrows,
created points on a timeline
constitute a life,
lived with presumed consequences.
A numerical designation of an age,
a page on a calendar
marks the edge, the event horizon
between the light and dark:
a mere point plotted in time and space—
and yet it matters.

Rome, the Eternal

Just one more pilgrim, disembarked
from luxury cruise ship, following a tour guide
through the eternal streets, slammed by crowds
of worshipers, nuns in habits, camera-wielding oglers,
Gypsy pickpockets, street musicians, and hawkers.
Everything for sale: Papal images, rosaries and icons,
Tee shirts and caps, canoli and cold drinks—From
spiritual mementos
to touristy trash, something for everyone.
The noise, the heat and humidity, the multitudes jostling,
jabbering
in polyglot syllables, chaos an infernal circle,
hordes trudging, sweating bodies colliding, Dantean.

The Vatican, the City of God on this side Tiber,
the mighty fortress walled by faith, dogma, and tradition,
epicenter of the Church of Rome.
Within the Basilica, epic grandeur, an edifice rising in
marble stateliness,
like angelic Hallelujahs in crescendo-ing stone
with grace notes of stained glass,
priceless artwork, statues and paintings, mosaics, sing to
the eyes
and souls of faithful like austere Gregorian chants
or resonant Renaissance harmonies, celebrating God and
Man.
Gaggles of tourists, whispering, snapping photos to
capture eternity
move among silent worshipers, kneeling wrapped in
contemplation.
Tucked in corners, the effigies of the faithful dead,
undisturbed, await in serenity.
And somewhere beneath the floor,
a simple Galilean Fisherman rests, removed by millennia

from the scurry and the madness,
(the distant footsteps of followers overhead,
the centuries of pilgrims)
that swirl through the tide of time.

Across town, separated by space and time and cultures,
the Coliseum rises in wrecked majesty,
pillaged victim of time and greed, still iconic ruins.
Camera-wielding tourists gawk
as guides' recitations of history and statistics
echo on the stones, the seats where fifty thousand sat
and cheered, lust slaked
by gladiators' blood poured forth as sacrifice on sand
to please the screaming crowd.
And now where docile pilgrims stroll,
the ghosts of Rome, its glory and its excess, drift like dust
in sunlight.

Beneath the streets and ruins, cathedrals and monuments,
strata of cultures crushed to dust,
Etruscan, Greek, and Roman,
sink to forgetfulness. The ordinary lives, art and
architecture,
forgotten gods and kings,
their Ozymandian splendor lost to history and time.
Tourists, marauding vandals, loaded with souvenirs,
with photographs and memories, the spoils of the day,
scurry to their waiting ship to a night of luxury
and dreams of Roman decadence.

Beneath their satiated somnolence,
singing them to slumber,
the whisper of the waves,
the wake of the Mediterranean parts white against the
hull.

The songs of antiquity, eternal call of the wine dark sea,
drifts across the waves.
The calls of drowned Phoenician sailors,
venturing out of sight of land,
the songs of helmed Etruscans ring like swords
on shields of bronze.
The epic chants of brave Achaians
call out, seeking revenge and glory
against the shattered walls of Troy,
and arrogant Odysseus heeding the Siren call,
but following the beacon of Penelope and home.
Centuries of voices, of cultures sunk to history,
layers of memory's collective consciousness
sing to sleepers drifting beyond Rome
to memories of greatness, the ghosts of emperors,
of warriors, of gods of cultures past.
The dark sea that gives and takes,
rolls on, restless as Neptune's dream,
eternal beyond the dreams of men.

Seasonal

Leaves fall, birds flying south reflect
a subtle seasonal temporal shift
as calendar and cosmos intersect:
describing arbitrary planetary drift.

Seismic
(For Monet)

Final journey done, a quiet house,
echoes of rippling silence.
Tectonic shifts, time tilts,
slips sideways, settles to aftershocks.
Memories and joys drift in corners,
patient as the abiding dust
settles, then swirls.
The crust of normalcy hardens.
Beneath, the molten lava surge,
wracked and restless, heaves;
rages of grief crack and bubble.

Shards of shattered memory,
cracked in Cubist planes,
rearrange reality.
Time flows and shifts in eddies:
the present time and tide we grasp
become the drifting past.

Epicenter of the seismic shift—
small blue urn on a pedestal,
the focus of love and loss,
cool, serene, though held,
rests untouched by time.

Silver
(For Deloris, on our Silver Anniversary)

A quarter of a century,
years of joy and passion,
of sorrows shared, of moments
that create a life together.

The burst of flame ignited
subdues to deeper glow,
transmutes the dross of ordinary life
to treasured memories.

The gleam of silver, purified,
encircles us, a halo,
the aura that surrounds our life,
fulfillment of the years.

Singularity

Her pupils dilate in dim light;
she gazes, wide-eyed and lost.
His unfamiliar face hovers, floats above.
He searches for the memories,
the girl she once had been
before plaques and synapses
snarled into Gordian confusions.

Their passions, like twin stars,
streamed plasma arcs, fueled by fusion,
across space—chaos and loneliness.
Joined, conjoined in cosmic dance,
shared desires fueled their cores.
But now her mind implodes,
swallowed in the singularity of despair.
Memories, the past, drift like dust
caught by the gravity of disease.
Thoughts and feelings wonder, wander
behind those eyes that peer past his.
She frowns, or smiles,
captive in an abyss of self.

He hovers, helpless,
at the edge of the edge,
an event horizon—
her pupils' stark darkness,
a profound eternal Night.

Stage Four

The room is cold and sterile.
Doctor enters, grim-faced,
clad in white, armed with stethoscope,
shielded by a clipboard and rationality.
Verdict couched in careful syntax
and polysyllabic Latinates,
pronounced—sentence hangs in the air.
Life and death deduced, reduced
to numbers and careful terminology.

Cells multiply beyond control,
irrational numbers, countdown,
inevitable subtraction of a life,
six to twelve.
Schedules and procedures
structure the treatments.
Chemo, medical oxymoron that kills to save.

Infusion room, rank and file,
patients queued up, reclined
supine, spiked by IV needles.
Steady drip drip drip
through tubing into veins,
pumped to lurking tumors
to mutated molecules of DNA.

Daily skirmish fought to stalemate,
across the board the opponent
moves pieces with a spectral hand.
Denial of *Zugzwang*, desperate
though sick to death,
retching and wretched,
staggering unbowed.

From day to day, the battles and the war,
taking the calculated risk,
stage four, the numbered days and months.
Word problems, an equation—
the mathematics of mortality,
factoring in the chemicals,
an equation, a solution
to combat the dissolution.

Winter: Two Poems

I. Desolation Angels

Desperation, abandoned hope,
black clouds drift, nimbus rumbles rise,
dark wings cast shadows
that move across the face of earth,
a pall on winter landscape.
Boreas whispers over trees,
appalling, stark as Dante's suicides.
Nature composes her winter dirge
from the thesaurus of despair.

II. Janu-Weary

Gray-cold dismal January days:
No lacy white or crystal flakes
to lighten winter bleak.
Red and green tucked away,
spring pastels still hibernate
beneath umber tones
of autumn's stark remains.

Among the whispering leaves
a flash, crimson-burst
of cardinal
breaks bleakness.
Warbling tones of wrens
brave blustering wind,
rattle of barebone branches.

A meager repast sustains fragile-feathered titmice,
sparrows, and chickadees.
They pick among the leaves
for errant seeds, withered berries,
gleaning the last harvest offerings.
Turning season's promise hovers,
still, unheard, beneath the dormant earth.

The Burden of Beauty

Broad face following the sun,
as calculus equations
rule its diurnal course.
Sunflower's phototropic arc
as pattern turns to pattern,
Fibonacci swirls project
galactic graphs, curving arms extend
and drift, a choreography
of synchronicity, the golden ratio.

As sunlight glows across her face,
Almond eyes examine cheekbones,
regarding flawless skin,
refracted images projected to the world
that does not see what she sees.
Reflected in silver symmetry, structural integrity
of proportional planes and angles,
geometry and genetics: aesthetics sculpt the curve.

Calculated patterns of curves and symmetry,
relative perfection of Structures into form.
Shades that flicker fluctuating shapes,
equations, algorithms grasp for meaning, for solutions.
Imperfect minds calculate, seek for absolutes
among variables irrational and undefined,
bear the burden of beauty
incalculable and Pure.

Mediterranean by Moonlight

She stands on un-breached battlements, alone,
The breeze caressing shoulders bare to night.
The wine-dark sea that murmurs to the shore
Lifts moored Achaean ships on lunar tides.

The tents stretch out across the sands below
As fires flicker, answering the stars.
The glint of arms and armor, silver-shine,
Made ghostly by the gleam of moonlight glow.

She lifts her silver flute to tender lips
And breathes across the aperture her breath
Transformed to notes, shaped by her fingertips,
A wistful whisper wafted on the breeze.

As music lifts and settles far below,
A web of sound drifts down to sleepers' ears,
A sibilant that soothes their dreams of war,
Reminding them of wives, of hearth and home.

Her husband, in his tent, his mournful dreams
Transmute to joyful memories of love
Till music fades like moonlit clouds at dawn.
She stands a moment, silent in the night.

Her life inconstant as the wanton orb
Adrift on shifting clouds, the ebb and flow
A melody, uncertain harmonies,
A chord (and discord) fading unresolved.

She turns, her pale feet slide across the stones,
Returning to her captor's loving arms.
Beauty and grace, desired and despised,
Her destiny deciding: love and war.

Gold

Gold-gleam of varnished wood grain glows,
as honeyed notes arise from quivering strings
caressed by fingers, touched by drawing bow.
Held in such an intimate embrace,
secure beneath his chin, his cradled palm,
she vibrates harmonies, her modulated tones,
exquisite peaks to thrilling lower notes
that resonate their rush across the skin.

Vivaldi's singing tones, a hymn to seasons' turns,
the fertile primavera rush
that drifts and swirls across the trilling notes,
the octave runs like garlands on the page.
From movement to movement they waltz,
united in the sound of passion's harmony.
Music and musician, the dancer and the dance,
fulfilled in their crescendo
the rush of Stradivarian romance.

Danse

The lights go up, uncertain choreography
of death and entrances,
we dance the jagged edge.
From cygnette dance to dying swan,
from pirouette *en pointe*
to swirl of graceful agonies.

From pas de deux of passions' interplay,
to clash of dissonance, regret, remorse.
Overture to final bow,
aubade to requiem.
The lights drop down, the curtain falls.

Like dandelion seeds, waft in the wind,
the last act and the first.
We dance in Kali's desperate waltz
of endings and beginnings.
Our firefly-flicker lives lived
at the speed of dark.

Getting Back to Normal

I

Chaos: order overturned
by the thousand un/natural shocks
the enemies of routine, of treasured normalcy.
Patterns, customary constructs
upset, scrambled jigsaw puzzle pieces
the picture tossed aside, awry.

Household appliances give in to entropy,
sick pets, a fall with broken hip and injured back
lead to unplanned treks:
the hardware store, the vet,
hospital Emergency.

Our best-laid plans,
patterns and structures swept aside,
flotsam and jetsam in a flood.
Floundering against the tide, the flow
of temporality, swept on amid debris
of fractured ordinary.

II

We search blaze-blurred,
looking up and out,
to sunlight's blinding light,
self-defeated in the search.
We listen to the voice of echoes
of our call for answers,
answering the overwhelming question
with another question.

Through physics, metaphysics,
through mathematics, myth, or magic,
we peer outward or within
for patterns in the random semaphore
of flash and pulse of distant lights.
We stare and squint,
at floral-whorl order
or Fibonacci swirls of the galaxies.
We listen for the Voice beyond,
ears turned to hear, intent
till silence turns to sound,
the flow of blood within
becomes the pattern that we seek.

We search for normal, order:
nor-mal, nor-bon, not bad or good.
The concept of a pattern, becomes a con
or a construct, of the Real.

Rose of Sharon

HIM: Oh, my love, she kisses me
    and her lips are honeyed, soft.
    Her breath like perfume, like sweet incense
    carries my heart aloft.

HER: My love stands strong, and he holds me close.
    I look in his adoring eyes.
    I lie content in his loving arms,
    to his touch my passions rise.

BOTH: Our love fills our souls like the bees'
    honeycomb,
    The sweetness is food for our hearts.
    Our passion a garden of plenty,
    From which we will never depart.

HIM: Her breasts like nestling turtledoves,
    her belly like heaps of wheat,
    the orchards of her fertile love
    fill me, leave me complete.

HER: His arms entwine around me
    like tendrils of fruited vines.
    Kisses intoxicate, entrance
    As cups of crimson wine.

BOTH: Our love fills our souls like the bees'
    honeycomb.
    The sweetness is food for our hearts.
    Our passion a garden of plenty,
    from which we will never depart.

HIM: She is my rose of Sharon,
HER: (I am his Rose of Sharon)
      as pure as lilies' bloom.
      (he holds my perfect bloom)
      The bouquet of her perfect love
      (he calls forth my perfect love)
      a heavenly perfume.
      (Our heavenly perfume).

BOTH: Our love fills our souls like the bees'
        honeycomb,
      The sweetness is food for our hearts.
      Our passion a garden of plenty,
      From which we will never depart.
      Our passion a garden of plenty,
      From which we will never depart.

Twilight of the Gods

Gotterdammerung

From the frigid depths of Jotunheim
the wrathful Frost Giants emerge,
their vengeance sweeps across the realms
in a tidal wave of battle surge.

The Wolf, freed from its chains and lair,
rips living flesh with slavering jaws,
destroying life and bringing death
with mortal fangs and claws.

REFRAIN:
The Ragnarok brings destruction,
chilling Realms with frigid breath
unless the might of Asgard's gods
can halt the dark of icy death.

From Ygradrasill, great Tree of Life,
roots and boughs throughout the universe are spread,
from Niflheim and Jotunnheim to Asgard,
encompassing the span of Time and Space
of what is past and what to come.

The Midgard Serpent, tearing at the roots
lies, baring envenomed fangs.
Its earth-encircling deadly coils
ensnare the Hammer-wielding Hero
in agony from poison's bitter pangs.

REFRAIN

The Bifrost, glittering Rainbow Bridge,
in shimmering shards Kaleidoscopes

beneath the steel of armored hooves,
great steeds that bear the Giant foe,
shattering the paths of human hope.

Nine Realms that span the Universe
in Chaos and Discord clash.
The universal Harmony, its balance swept aside
by the Frost Giants' discordant violence,
as light and warmth of life implode
in blinding Apocalyptic Flash.

REFRAIN

The Dark and Cold of Death descend
into the Reign of Night.
But Hope remains to hear the strains
of Harmony once more,
a glimmer of new Light.

Then from the Dark and Silence
a Spark, a Note shall arise, restoring all.
Odin, the All-Father, awakening from sleep,
crescendo-ing of light and life
in Trumpet's clarion Call.

REFRAIN

The Ragnarock brings destruction,
The Gotterdammerung,
chilling Realms with frigid death,
until the light of Asgard's risen god
restores the living harmony
with the Voice, music's reviving breath.
Restores the living harmony
With the Voice, music's reviving breath.

Krishna and the Milkmaids

Milkmaids
With flowing hair and flashing eyes, they dance.
They guide their lowing herds to verdant fields.
They sway like wafting breezes over grass,
their laughter like the blossoms opening.
The gopis sing, their gentle voices lilt,
chanting and enchanting as they swirl
among the grazing cows they twist and turn,
entrance the gentle god who watches them.
Refrain
The harmonies of joy, the sacred choreography
enchants, entices lovers, opposites entwine,
becoming one, the blissful unity
of Kama Sutra's mystical embrace.
Krishna
He plays his flute, touches the apertures,
the notes drift like the butterflies, touching Radha's ears.
She pauses, turns, and smiles at his gaze.
She swirls, her iridescent dress flashes in the light.
She moves, responding to the notes he plays.
His soft breath whispers to his bamboo flute
that weaves a spell, the choreography
for Radha and the milkmaids' joyful feet.
Refrain
Milkmaids
Encircling her dance, attendants swirl,
their flashing feet and flowing arms entice
her devotee to join her in the dance,
to play his notes, to move to her embrace
within their circle's unifying charm.
The dancers and the dance combine and lift
and drop together on the sacred notes
that fade to stillness on the whispered breeze.
Refrain

Still

Hospital cubicle, a pale cocoon,
machines whir and click, a clock ticks unheard
as time and space compress and pause
around the tableau on the elevated bed.
She rests supine, still beneath the sheets
cradling the swaddled form.
Her fingers smooth his hair,
lips breathe into fragile folds.
Cheek pressed to cheek, salt tears glisten,
christening cerulean blue porcelain skin.

Beneath full breasts, a heart in jagged shreds
mutters palpitations, whispers grief
to inattentive ears.
Hands caress and clutch, small form moves
on the rise and fall, the waves of loss.

Outside the door, attendant angels in blue scrubs, hover,
their sturdy limbs and hands
more confident before emergencies,
shattered limbs, spouting blood,
the charted symptoms, diagnoses
of desperate mortality.

Their soft insistent voices
break the spell, pry her grasping fingers.
Muscle memory holds the phantom infant,
consoling hands touch, distract
as he is spirited away.

Her heart a gulch ripped wide,
gave him flesh and form
 and, briefly, life.
Madonna coalesces into Pieta.
She clings to love and pain,
Her son gone, but with her
Still.

Fourth Dementia

Times Square revelers, restless throng,
exhaled breath a cloud.
Upward gaze toward crystal ball,
flashing facets fall.
Calendar and clock, time squared, conspire
as hour, day, and year wind down
to arbitrary end
as the year runs out of time.

The clock behind me whispers,
the second hand a nervous tic,
gestures, talks of entropy.
Champagne bubbles rise
and disappear.
The flash of lights and lives,
a moment come and gone,
like lemmings we await the starting gun.
The flashing facets fall.

While overhead, the galaxy,
the sweep of space and time,
the ebb and flow drift
measureless, unmeasured.
The flux and silence comprehend,
knowing and unknown.

DESIGN

I
From strands of DNA, from patterns,
chemical equations threaded into cells,
she flings her fragile filaments
across space and time, from branch to branch,
uncertain as the breeze that wafts it.
Her dark, unlovely bulbous shape
emits the fragile thread
and weaves it in a paradigm.
Embedded in her being, the algorithm,
the aesthetics of design, complicated calculus,
the one pattern that she knows
astonishes and captivates the mind
in a web of gossamer beauty,
deadly by design.

II
Drifting from unsubstantial clouds,
vapor lifted up, transfigured form to form,
and floating, shaped by frigid air
icy fingers shape each drop
to crystalline geometry,
each unique,
in a blizzard of beauty,
patterns on patterns float and swirl,
an icy choreography,
the music of the wind sweeps in drifts and flows.
Profligate beauty appears and moves
and melts, the moment come and gone
before the melting sun,
leaving wonder, fascination
meditating on design.

Arachne

Flung filaments against the glass, cast upon the breeze,
entangle trees and clouds.
Spun silk patterns, beaded, crystal droplets tremble,
reflect the world.

She hunches in the center,
eight legs sprawled,
unloved if not unlovely,
in the web she scribbled from herself.
The brown pod that she guards,
filled with her arachnid progeny.

She clenches against the breath,
she stretches forth to feel
struggles against the tensile strength.
She sidles forth, settles beside the victim,
selects the spot
then plunges fangs to sip the life.

Somewhere within the poppyseed brain
the DNA lurks, the template
that directs her spinnerets,
her spindle legs and agile feet,
tatting the threads, complex geometry
of delicate death.

Patient in the center of her vibrating web
entangling the world,
fulfilled in the necessity
to weave, to feed and breed
and pass the threads, the helix
before untangling, dropping the stitches,
the warp and woof of life.

Έκσταση

Beauty beyond desire,
beyond casual profligate excesses—
like transient flashes of color among trembling leaves
as buds burst forth to petulant petals
that drift to dust below.

As lightning arcs in shards
that shatter against dark clouds
and paralyze, shuddering to stillness
our exhalation by its force,
like stepping forth from Plato's Cave
from darkness into light;

As wheeling stars and galaxies
draw us up and out, beyond
the temporal imperfections,
the casual chaos of ordinary life;

The Pieta, in luminescent stone,
transforms the grief
of death, a mother's tears,
the child she bore now bears
in silent tragedy, sublime repose.

Bernini's saint surrenders
to the archangel's insouciant smile,
his casual offhand touch entices
her to ecstasy, head back, lips parted,
anticipating the release
beyond desire.

As fire transmutes,
dissolves impurities, passion transforms
by ecstasy
to serene perfection.
The Golden Mean, eternal Harmonies remain,
the gravitas beyond the weight
of ordinary dross.

Sign of Loss

**For Koko the Gorilla
(4 July 1971-19 June 2018)**

Her deep-set amber eyes shift and search
behind eyelids creased with age.
Her nostrils flare, the whisper of her breath irregular,
sniffing,
    snuffling,
her breathing stops
  and starts.
Her bulk uneasy,
limbs stretched, then still.
Eyes move again.
Her great hands flex as fingers twitch.

What scenes roll like film behind her eyes?
What tactile memories stimulate her nerves,
her simian brain?
What dreams may come?
    Born in captivity,
does some dim racial memory
  of lowland forests sway among synapses,
a prelapsarian paradise,
    the sounds, the scents, the tastes
of bird calls and succulent, sweet fruit?

Broad thick-nailed phalanges, foreshortened opposable thumbs
  reach out, palms up to some unseen ancestral clasp.
Her fingers move, a memory, signs perhaps
    like whispers to her past,
finger bracelet, tickle Koko, AllBall, a lost kitten
  (cuddle replacement for maternal disappointment).

She reaches up to touch her eyes, sweeping down her cheeks,
   a memory of loss.
Final movements, twitching fragments
  like half-spoken whispered words.
Muscles relax, an exhaled breath--
  Release--
    Her fingers still.
The final sign is silence.

Electric Blue

Late August sun charges cerulean dome,
heat blazes down the spectrum—
glowing infrared to ultraviolet.

Sounds shimmer in the air,
cicada buzz crescendos,
                tautness intensifies,
then fades, pauses,
                  vibrates in ripples
like dopplered waves
across the rising heat.

Bumble bees fumble petals,
plunge to pollen,
   hum stirs,
      vibrant plants respond
to fecund afterglows.

Iridescent emerald wings, ruby throats whir.
    Rainbow intensities zip,
   feathered susurrations,
      flash, then gone.

The heat of afternoon
settles, muffles and dampens,
stifling sounds to quiet dusk.
As bright blue deepens into indigo,
     crickets chirp,
          persistent katydids
fill the loud bright night.
   Wings, legs rub, vibrate intensities
     darkness alive, a humming counterpoint
to cool stars and moonlight summons.

Night settles into quiet,
    fulfilled.
Persistent memories melt and fade,
  darkness deepens,
    perchance to dreamless silence
as they await the rising sun.

Loss and Memory
(For Jane Elizabeth and Ginny Lynn)

Weathered granite block, engraved,
Two names, two years, two sisters, first and last of six—
they rest together, one an unknown presence, gone before,
the other a wavering image, a mirage,
a jewel-box consigned to silence in the earth.

Those who still remember
stand in attendance, held by the gravity of loss
then join them, one by one.
She who would have held them,
kissed their sleeping eyes,
watched them grow,
now rests beside them, swaddled,
asleep beyond the sweep of time.

Through decades of my life,
Their presence, a wisp of thought,
Not quite a memory, has whispered through synapses.
The brother that I might have been to them
walks from the country churchyard,
carries the loss
and leaves them,
but bears the stillness of memory.

Knapping Stones

Forged in the furnace—raging heat
of volcanic magma flow
cast forth to cool,
its gleaming planes reflect the firelight
in the sheltering cave.

Hammerstone chips flakes,
shapes edge to biface curve.
The old-stone artisan grasps obsidian,
knobby, thick-nailed fingers touch and turn
the flashing lithic artifact,
fashioned to hard-edged death.
Spearhead or arrow shaped to pierce
thick hides, open crimson fountains,
bring thunderous defeat to megafauna prey.

Flesh becomes flesh.
Then predator and prey drift down to dust
through sands of millennia.
Time and history coalesce,
as hands now plunge through centuries,
dig down and back to touch, connect
with bones and objects buried, lost.

Paleontologist hefts the spearhead,
tests the razor edge, rubs the beveled surfaces.
Obsidian heated and heaved from the cauldron
of the shaping infant earth,
then crafted by gnarled fingers
to lie in wait in mortal drift.

The knapped stone passes on,
down through centuries by hands now dust,
to curious modern grip,
threaded by double helix strands,
a baton relayed in the human race
against time.

Now and Zen
Haiku Meditations

Clouds on calm water
drift above, reflect below
rippling, still, untouched

Orion rising
drawing gold-gleam clouds behind
Harbingers of day

I hear the water.
Do you hear the grasshopper
which is at your feet?

Our saline blood's pulse
floods through our veins, ocean tides:
ebb and flow of life.

Lips on aperture,
bamboo flute recalls the breeze,
whispered memories.

Dimensionless point
center of the spinning world
contemplates the Tao.

Complex harmonies—
music unifies our minds:
Many and the One.

Tai Chi: strength and grace—
sweep clouds, move heaven and earth—
peaceful Qigong flow.

Food for Thought

"You're a vegan. What do you eat?"
She asked me in the Publix produce section.
We stood in the Edenic abundance,
A cornucopia of splendor.
Mounds of vibrant apples, tempting red and green.
Peaches smooth and fragrant as a lover's cheek,
Salads rich in textures, verdant green and blushing reds.
Bell peppers gleaming green, yellow, red, and orange.
Potatoes, earthy roughness, humble brown,
Recline against sweet orange yams.
Eggplants in midnight purple sleekness,
Beans in rainbow hues—red, white, browns, and blacks,
Snuggle in cozy jumbles, legumes bearing life.

An orgy of tastes, delights
Filling every sense, arousing, fulfilling needs
For sensual delights and nourishment.
I stand entranced by food
Enticing taste buds, eyes, and nose.
I smile back at her,
I gesture large and nod.

Drift

Winter dark and cold:
the planetary shift and flow through space,
the axis tilts through revolutions.
Days lengthen, morning clouds
tinted by the glow of rising sun.
Buds burst to leaves
as blossoms swell to fruit.

Birds harken to the chromosomal charge,
selecting twigs and bits of fluff
to weave their nests and procreate,
to be fruitful and multiply.
The days are filled with song,
mating calls and territory claims.:
high-pitched cicada buzz,
the nights with calls of katydids
and cricket chirps,
the silent flash of fireflies.

The days' diurnal spiral:
fledglings grow and leave the nest.
Fruits ripen to succulent flesh,
as leaves shift down the spectrum,
prismatic biochemistry of green
to red, then brown.

Blue skies deepen,
days grow short, as white clouds darken, drop.
The seasons change through planetary shift
of orbit and axial tilt,
drifting toward some cosmic end
of chaos and entropy.

On the Inevitability of Entropy

The body needs:
It feeds and breeds,
until at last
it pushes weeds.

Spring Morning after Rain: Impressions

Pastel flashes of bird song
notes swirl, blend in morning Monet swathes of sound.
Vivaldi sings in trills,
in pinks, whites, magentas--
azaleas, dogwoods in symphonies, green glissando.
Passions, rebirth, riots of sound and color flash
celebrate the fling of life
across the morning sky.

Solstice

Sun's orange disc escapes from bare-branch clutch
   to slip below horizon curve
and leave Earth to cold and dark.
  Beyond the ecliptic swerve
     and depths of spacetime
blaze-bright suns star-twinkle.

The red-shift bend of light refracts,
    responds to twinkling Christmas lights
entwined in evergreens.
Menorah candles aligned, marshalled
   against the cold and Dark.
Yule logs spark from flicker-flames,
   glowing heat, casting shadows
loom and dance.

We huddle, looking up and out,
ancestral memories lurk
The bleak-black cold—icy fingers touch,
  numb our shivered flesh
with mortal dread.

Along the ecliptic,
Planetary axial tilt, bent
  from the light and warmth,
    wobbles in its parabolic path.
The small blue marble rolls in darkness
  around the stellar blaze
a pilgrimage toward light and warmth,
returns to life,
  the path to vernal equinox.

I Am Bic

I am a ballpoint pen.
I am, like Whitman, multitudes, a collage, a jumble
Thoughts and experiences, a lava lamp.
I am colors, red and gray and black, chiaroscuro
On a page, my poems.
    I am flowing water and stirring breeze
        That move leaves on surfaces
           Like thoughts in verses, leaves of grass.
I am a swirl of images
                Of rhymes and sounds
That drift down pages,
        Lines that shift
             As ideas move, connect
From verse to verse
        Better or worse.
Beginnings and endings shift and change.
Until the last resounding couplet
Crescendos, bringing down
    the movement, symphony of verse
        that sings aloud
I Am.

Maternity
(For Amanda and Nora)

Beneath the fecund autumn sun
that gilds the gold-gleam leaves,
three generations, and one in utero,
surround, enfold and celebrate another life.
Babies dandled on generous laps,
held to expansive breasts,
they balance plates of pastel cake,
frosting fluffy as cumulus clouds.

Laughter and voices drift,
and wrapping paper rustles
from opened gifts, dresses and shoes,
receiving blankets and ribbons
to welcome new life,
offerings to the new Madonna.
One hand on lower back,
one curved beneath the swell of life she carries.

Husbands hover at the edges,
uncertain but aware,
like attendants to the priestesses
at a ceremony,
a ritual, supporting secondary roles,
they offer drinks and food,
communion gifts to celebrate maternity.

Generation to generation,
mother to daughter, back through distant past,
passing on through chromosomes,
mitochondrial strands, umbilicus
uniting female life to life.
Back to Willendorf to Lucy,
back to Mother Eve.
Back to the plains of Africa
or the Garden's fertile soil.
The life that flows like milk and honey,
the river springs, unites:
Headwaters of humanity, the Source,
Mother Goddess of the race.

Abject

Late October, un-sheaved corn
shivers, withered leaves whisper,
importuning dark and silent drifting clouds.
Ragged sunlight staggers across patchwork fields.

Tattered scarecrow, faded face forlorn,
straw protrudes, ripped stitches gape.
head down, arms outstretched,
resigned to impotence and entropy
of declining days.

Gleaming crows pick through stubble,
corvid congregants bow,
glean the sparse repast: scant remaining kernels,
harvest's last communion.

Clouds deepen, stretch toward the east.
The sun shifts away
as the horizon rolls
toward night and winter cold.

Guernica

Apocalyptic angels bear the emblem
Of the crooked cross, rain screaming fire
From late afternoon clouds.
Upturned faces shriek, echoing the death
That falls, smashing walls and lives,
A Cubist collage of stained glass shattered
To glittering bits.

Mother bears a lifeless child
Through smoke, the iron stench of death
Wafts a halo overhead.
The fallen warrior's broken sword,
Useless in the dust, offers surrender,
Clutched in grasping claw.
A chorus of dying animals,
Pale horse and tawny bull,
ripped by shrapnel
Like a picador's probing lance,
Their fading moans disharmony
of chaos and destruction.

The swooping wings depart
Into the dying light.
In the end was the word,
And the word was death, destruction,
Mors Vobiscum,
And the unrest is silence.

Tunnel Visions

I
We lie together, touching silvered skin,
shimmer from the wanton voyeur moon,
the breeze stirs the curtains,
stroking fingers shivering vibrato on the skin.
Breaths and whispered sentiments,
harmonies of voices rise
pianissimo, to appassionato,
crescendo-ing to silence.
Movement and thrust, muscles grip, release,
dilated pupils empty into one another,
the abyss of otherness.

II
Birth pangs spasm-thrust,
pressures compress, release
from comforting darkness to first light.
The gateway dilates,
amniotic christening,
unused lungs expand, in-
spired to breathe, first gasp
expels a primal protest.
Muscles flex as inch worm fingers grasp
and soft lips seek the waiting breast.
Warm hands guide and comfort,
ease the trauma of expulsion into life.

III
The end whispers finale to attentive ears,
deaf to other voices, other sounds
of machines working to forestall
the inevitable end.
Fingers smooth, then clutch cool sheets,
gesturing to the Other,
fondling One who waits.
The room silent, as others watch,
attendants, voyeurs unaware, unsure.

Eyes open, search the ceiling,
dilate, gaze sightless,
as muscles, hands spasm and release.
Breath exhales, ex-spires,
into a light of tunnel visions.

Three Score and Ten
19 September 2019

As morning sun ignites a crimson flush
and dapples whispering leaves like tongues of flame,
the Hunter strides across the galaxy,
and parallels my own foreshortened arc.

I stand, face lifted to the morning song,
enchanted by the blush of shifting clouds.
I feel the years, the memories extend
behind me, a parade of seasons passed
that pushes me to the horizon's edge
to face the dawn, confront the tick of time.
The cusp of signs and seasons curves away
as Maiden yields to Libra's balanced scales.

As summer's blaze gives way to autumn's glow
and growth yields to the harvest's fruitfulness,
I pause, transfixed in lambent radiance.
The sweep of days and years, the swath of life
fulfills itself in seasons' turning tide.

Reviews of *String Theory* and *Wind Song*

String Theory

"Dr. Covel's poetry reminds me of the poetry of William Butler Yeats. . . a glimpse into a very talented poet's mind—his pensive and expansive vocabulary, his references to many historical people and places, and his knowledge of life."
Anita Buice, *Times-Georgian*

"The poems are very subtle and understated. They don't grab me by the throat the way that, say, Dylan Thomas' work can grab me by the throat. Instead, they plant their seeds very subtly, and find certain lines popping back into my mind days or weeks after I've read them. They stick with you, like something whispered."
Jeff Suwak, author of *Beyond the Tempest Gate*

Wind Song

Reading Robert Covel's poetry is a double treat. In "Wind Song," the poet's second collection of his works, calm and reassurance dominate his observations and lyrical lines even as you embark on a great journey of imagistic pleasure and intellectual incitement. . . . Take up "Wind Song" and do just as the author does: call up a relaxing tune or classical tome, read and let the songs of these poems lift you into a land of remarkable images, reassurance and pleasure.
Chuck Wanager, author of *Taking Our Love Offline*, a collection of poetry; *Jackson Flats*, a novel; and *Play Sgt. Pepper One More Time*, a memoir.

WIND SONG is erudite, cerebral, yet amazingly accessible. It is thought-provoking as well as entertaining. The language is beautiful, overflowing with appropriate comparisons, images, and sensory details. Make sure to read the poem aloud to hear the music.

 Dr. Eleanor Wolfe Hoomes, author of *Bread and Roses, Too*, *The Eye of the Beholder*, *Green Thumbs*, and *Driving with My Blinker On*.

Acknowledgments

Writers are a part of a community, as well as a part of the cosmos that inspires us. My community gives more than I can say. I wish to thank the members of the Carrollton Creative Writers Guild and especially the members of Just Poetry for their constant suggestions and feedback. I wish to thank friends and fellow writers Claudia Kennedy, Dr. Eleanor Wolfe Hoomes and Dr. Cecilia Lee for reading everything and offering encouragement. Thanks to Frank Allan Rogers for our on-the-road conversations about writing. Val Mathews is editor extraordinaire, and her suggestions turned some decent poems into real worthwhile poetry. I want to thank Alistair Riddoch, my Facebook friend who created the cover design, giving one of my haikus a visual reality that expresses my world view.

I want to thank my wife Deloris for being my first reader, supporting and believing in me and my work.

And to my readers, thank you for paying attention. Together we can use words to reshape the world.

www.ingramcontent.com/pod-product-compliance
Lightning Source LLC
Chambersburg PA
CBHW060331050426
42449CB00011B/2725